G340 Publishing, 7115 N Division St. Suite B #132, Spokane, WA 99208
Printed in the United States of America
First G340 Publishing printing March 2010.
www.g340.com

ISBN: 978-0-9843837-2-6

This book is dedicated to our central core, our own inner stone that grounds us, motivates us, drives us and keeps us going. Love, Faith, Family, Hope, Joy, Sadness, Fear. To that moment when we overturned and revealed something more within ourselves.

Live | Laugh | Love

The First Stone Overturned

by Gerald Ealy

Contents

A Moment 2

Love Is 4

The Raven and the Wolf 6

The Empty Side of the Bed 8

Passion 10

Break Away 12

You 14

I Have the Lord to Guide Me 16

Spring 18

Breathe 20

As I Lie Awake Tonight 22

Dreaming 24

I Love You 26

I Had a Dream That You Were Mine 28

Faces 30

Sometimes 32

My Only Love 34

Smile 36

Seashell 38

Are You the Other Part of My Heart 40

The Engineer 42

Follow Your Bliss 44

A Moment

There is a moment in the day,
when it is quiet and still.

There is a moment in the day,
when I am humbled and filled.

There is a moment in the day,
when I no longer feel alone.

There is a moment in the day,
when my true heart is known.

There is a moment in the day,
when I am whole again.

There is a moment in the day,
I don't have to pretend.

There is a moment in the day,
when everything is new.

That moment of the day,
is when I am finally with you.

Love Is

Love is a promise.
Love is letting go.
Love is holding on.
Love is patience.
Love is saying "no".
Love is saying "yes".
Love is commitment.
Love is walking away.
Love is giving.
Love is acceptance.
Love is a trickster.
Love is Faith.
Love is devotion.
Love is a circle.
Love burns you, frees you, raises you, and defeats you.
Love crushes you, evolves you, scars you and completes you.

The Raven and the Wolf

One night a raven followed the plaintive cry of a wolf, as its lonely howl echoed in the wilderness.
"Why do you cry so?" asked the raven.
"I call out to my love, for she is far from me and my heart longs to be with her" he replied.
"Why not simply join her? I have seen her not far from here across the river" said the raven.

The wolf cried out yet again and his voice traveled through the night air. In the distance his call was answered.
The raven hopped to a new branch, "Again you cry out, and you know she is not far".

The wolf turned to the raven, "It is not the distance -- my cry is for her and only her. When she hears me, she knows that even when we are not together, my heart joins hers" explained the wolf. "We must all be apart from the ones we love at times, but my love knows no distance, that is not the thunder, but my heart, that is not a river but my tears. For I shed them in the sadness when she is not here and I shed them for the joy she brings me when she returns".

The raven pondered the words of the wolf and shed his own tear.

"I did not know of such love until now. I shall think of my own love when I hear your cry and beat my wings harder to return, thank you friend".

The chorus of the wolves filled the air, carried on moonlight and love.

The Empty Side of the Bed

I wondered when I could face that side,
without the pain of what was said.
I wondered how I was still open wide,
when I touched the empty side of the bed.

I wondered when I would sort it out,
with just the silence now left instead.
I wondered how I am still in doubt,
when I touched the empty side of the bed.

I wondered when I should breathe again,
without the touch of my beloved.
I wondered how to stop the rain,
when I touched the empty side of the bed.

Passion

I feel the urge within me,
like a tide that never ends.
Your eyes have finally opened,
and the passion burns again.

You beckon and come toward me,
to embrace my eager frame.
With a flick of flying satin,
we fan desire's flame.

The breathing of our bodies,
starts to find a different beat.
The pace is ever building,
keeping time upon the sheet.

The sounds of our desire,
crescendos to a peak.
Immersed in loving climax,
that leaves us feeling weak.

And in the quiet minutes,
that follow from our soaring.
The sun slips through the curtain,
to tell us it is morning.

Your hand has but to touch me,
and I rise up with the sun.
The music starts to play.
Another concert has begun.

Break Away

Break away, young one, break away.

Your day of awakening is showing the way.
To find your future and treasures untold,
to find that your streets are all paved in gold.
Don't worry about us - it's the best for you,
to find all you can about what you can do.

Break away, young one, break away.

The lessons you've learned shall help you through life,
hopefully easing the pain and the strife,
that we all must face when we enter the world -
completely open, our wings unfurled.

Break away, young one, break away.

You

You are in my thoughts, though not in my arms.
You are in my dreams, though not in my sight.
You are in my heart, though it beats alone.
You are in my days, though we are apart.
You are in my nights, though the dawn comes too soon.
You are in my life, though I am alone.

You are in my soul, though I do not show it.
You are in my hopes, though I do not say it.
You are in my love, though you can not know it yet.

I Have The Lord to Guide Me

No matter what the trouble,
no matter how bad things may be,
I know within my heart and soul,
I have the Lord to guide me.

In times of sorrow and sadness,
when I feel I'm no longer free,
I look toward heaven, and then I know,
I have the Lord to guide me.

As I travel the road of life,
to tomorrows still untold.
I feel His presence along the way,
'till the days when I grow old.

Through those long years to come,
I'll face times of doubt and despair,
but all wounds heal and pain will fade,
for I know that He is there.

Wherever I may go in life,
to desert, to mountains, to sea.
I know that forever more,
I have the Lord to guide me.

Spring

You are that first rain of Spring,
that warm and gentle breeze,
carrying the scent of earth and sky.

You are that silent moment after waking but not awake,
when your mind still half dreaming,
cozy and safe between the sheets.

You are a hearth and home,
sweet smells of bread,
that easy, simple place.

You are my love,
for my heart beats faster,
when I see your face.

Breathe

There was a time when we were all small. Everything was just beyond our reach - the cookie on the counter, the toy at the top of the closet.

As we have gotten older we then discover that we are still reaching.

Something is always just beyond our reach - that new car, that promotion, that man or woman we think we want or need, reaching for something that drives us forward.

We try so hard that we forget to breathe.

We wonder why, if we are trying and doing our best to get whatever it is, that we are so exhausted in the effort.

We have forgotten to breathe - to support ourselves in the most basic and simple ways.

If you think back when you were small and what you did to get the cookie, you will find that you stopped and thought about it, you looked for the resources and the support you had to achieve that goal of chocolatey goodness.

Maybe it was a chair, maybe it was a sister or brother. But you stopped and took a deep breath and figured out your next step.

So breathe.

As I Lie Awake Tonight

As I lie awake tonight,
I wonder of His plan;
of how He shapes the world around me,
and moves the sea and sand.
I wonder how I play a part;
how I am guided by His hand.

As I lie awake tonight,
my eyes begin to close.
My mind finds peace and solace,
for all my thoughts He knows.
My fears and worry drift away,
and my mind finds its repose.

As I lay asleep tonight,
I dream of worlds untold;
of how He shapes my dreams around me,
and I see the world unfold.
I dream how I can be a better man,
how I fit into His plan.

As I rise to greet the day,
my heart is fill with gladness;
of how He shows the path before me,
free of fear and madness.
I walk the path within the light,
and see my dreams take flight.

Dreaming

When I dream of you,
of kisses and caresses,
of the blush of the rush
when our hearts beat and meet.

there is no time or space
just a place where we are one.

no noise.

Save for the breathless joy
of moans and tones
both deep and soft
that send our souls aloft.

That ecstasy of skin.

A journey from within
that ends with you.
When I dream of you.

I Love You

I love you more than chocolate.
I love you more than pie.
I love you for the little things,
no need to ask me why.
I love you for your smile.
I love you for your grace.
I love you more than the day before,
I can't wait to see your face.
I love your head,
and I love your toes,
and all the bits between,
I love you for who you are,
not who you might have been.

I Had a Dream You Were Mine

I had a dream that you were mine,
but only for a time, no time.
For hearts are fickle with the mind,
and choose a path to find.

The dream continued slow and fast,
sometimes future sometimes past.
All throughout a Love that lasts,
a warm deep glow it cast.

I had a dream that you were mine,
but only for a time, no time.
For hearts are fickle with the mind,
and choose a path to find.

And then the dream became so dark,
and the path became obscured.
The glow of Love was dimmed in black,
that I lost my way for sure.

I had a dream that you were mine,
but only for a time, no time.
For hearts are fickle with the mind,
and choose a path to find.

Then when I thought all was lost,
I closed my eyes and listened.
For your heartbeat as my beacon,
In my mind Love reappeared and glistened.

I had a dream that you were mine,
but only for a time, no time.
For hearts are fickle with the mind,
and choose a path to find.

I found you in the darkness there,
our Love came through to bind us

I know now to close my eyes,
for Love will always find us.

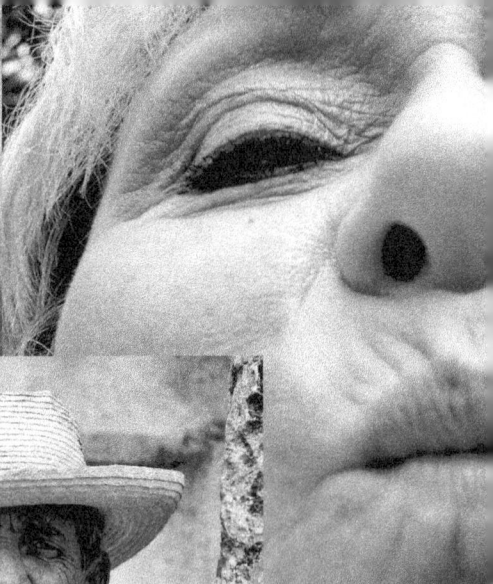

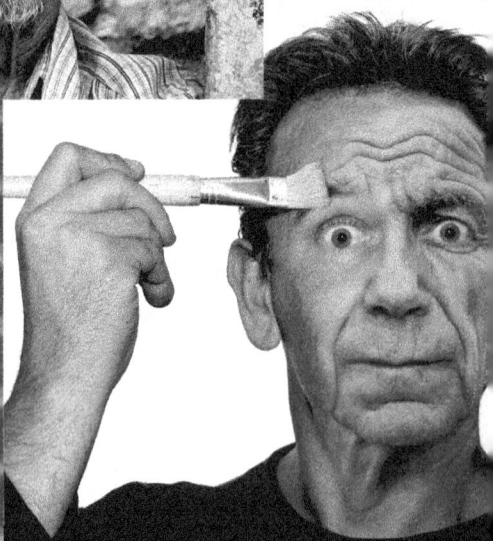

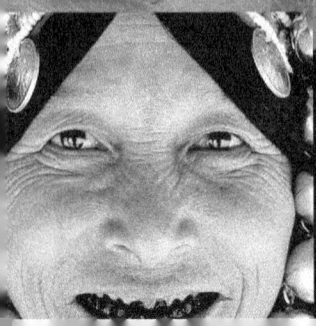

Faces

The face is like a tapestry of the soul.
Each thread of our life brings more detail and beauty.
Each line is a story, both happy and sad.
Every face is a new piece to the cloth of Humankind.
Unique.
A treasure.
Don't change, or rearrange, you have earned those lines.
Don't hide them, embrace them – they are your story of your time.

Sometimes

Sometimes when my strength is gone,
I find it there again with you.

Sometimes when its all gone wrong,
I find it right again with you.

Sometimes when the darkness comes,
I find the light again with you.

Sometimes I try with all my might,
I find more will again with you.

Sometimes the days are too long,
I find them short again with you.

Sometimes my voice can't find the song,
I find it there again with you.

There again with you, sometimes it's all I need.

My Only Love

You are my sunshine,
that brightens my day.
You are my direction,
that shows me the way.
You are my comfort,
when I am in sorrow.
You are my hope,
in each new tomorrow.
You are my strength
in times I am weak.
You are my dreams,
which I see in my sleep.
You are the one,
who will always be there.
You are so special,
for I know that you care.
You are an angel,
sent from above,
You are the only one,
I want to love.

Smile

A smile on your face, and a smile in your heart,
are always the good makings of a smile to impart.
So share a smile with loved-ones or just a simple friend.
For a smile is where the long friendships begin.

Seashell

As I was walking the beach one day,
with a seashell in my hand.
I remembered how I found it there,
buried beneath the sand.
Within its beauty found a sound,
which brought a peace into my mind.
The ocean waves merely washing away,
the love I could not find.
The sound that I heard was you my love.
Your voice and yours alone.
Harmonizing softy now,
with the great, deep ocean's tone.
Then the tide began to turn,
and the love returned to me.
And since that time I've been with you,
you've shown what love could be.

Are You the Other Part of My Heart?

I listen to the beat,
but something's incomplete.
Are you the other part of my heart?
I've been searching for so long,
to find the final notes to my song.
Are you the other part of my heart?
It's a chance that I'm taking,
on the new Love that we are making.
Are you the other part of my heart?
It feels right, it feels right, it feels right.
I need more than just a feeling,
'cause it's my heart with which we're dealing.
Are you the other part of my heart?
I know not to go too fast,
from the heartache in the past.
Are you the other part of my heart?
I need to have your trust,
and not give in to lust.
Are you the other part of my heart?
I don't know, I don't know, I don't know.
But I am ready to try.

The Engineer

He sits and he dreams of what he will be,
a wooden train for company.
Within his world he's an engineer,
through the dress shoe mountains he must steer.
From there he desends to the bedroom plain,
his room is the world for him and his train.
Grandfather has told him of the trains long ago,
as they sounded their whistles and let the steam blow.
He gave him the toy with which he now plays,
and the dream stays alive from old yesterdays.
The boy rounds the corner, to the train's last stop.
Which consists of a glass and some spilled soda pop.
Father comes in, for it's time for bed.
The little engineer falls asleep, as a story is read.
Each one of us has a goal to achieve,
to put our trust into a dream to believe.
Though each may have one's special theme,
we all deep inside have a boyhood dream.

Follow Your Bliss

Follow your bliss to that first stone overturned,
to live and breathe and know what you've learned.

Follow your bliss like an explosion above,
to never hold back on what you truly love.

Follow your bliss for it is yours alone,
to discover the mystery of that first stone.

Follow your bliss to listen to your core,
to acknowledge that wonder like never before.

Follow your bliss to the path light and dark,
to ignite the fire with your passion's spark.

Follow your bliss to that first stone overturned,
to live and breathe and know what you've learned.

Current titles available

House Shaking Sheep

The First Stone Overturned

Titles Coming Soon

Tinker

Grandma's Attic

www.ingramcontent.com/pod-product-compliance
Lightning Source LLC
Chambersburg PA
CBHW021920040426
42448CB00007B/832